HOW CANADA
GOT ITS CAPITAL

From their lusty beginnings as tough lumber towns, Ottawa and Hull have developed into modern cities which provide a unique urban environment. Our National Capital Area reflects the romance of our history and the vitality of our cultures.

Over the years, the development of the National Capital Area has been a remarkable demonstration of Canadian federalism in action. The development of Ottawa and Hull particularly in recent years, is showing us what can be done when governments work together to provide a better place for people to live.

It is because of my own feelings of pride and affection for our Capital that I am particularly pleased to see the publication of this beautiful book. Its fascinating story can now be shared by young Canadians across the nation.

Pierre Elliott Trudeau

HOW CANADA GOT ITS CAPITAL

Text by Nadja Corkum
Illustrations by Emma Hesse

Published in association with
The National Capital Commission
by McClelland and Stewart Limited

Reprinted 1976

The National Capital Commission,
48 Rideau Street, Ottawa.

McClelland and Stewart Limited
The Canadian Publishers
25 Hollinger Road, Toronto.

0-7710-2285-9

Printed and bound in Canada

In the Time of Champlain

Samuel de Champlain, explorer from France, was resting in his canoe and gazing at the silvery waterfalls which, from the middle of the Ottawa River, looked like two sheer, delicate curtains wafted on the summer breeze. It was June 4th, 1613, and he and his small group had been paddling up the River of the Algonquins, as Champlain called it, for eighteen days. But Champlain had not come to admire the falls. He was looking for something much more important: a Northwest Passage to India and China.

In those days, all explorers hoped to find the Northwest Passage. No one really knew for sure if it existed but, if it were discovered, the merchants of Europe would save a great deal of time and money. Carrying tea, silk or spices from the Far East home to Europe meant a long and dangerous journey around the continent of Africa. It could take as long as three years, and could end in tragedy when the flimsy sailing ships of those days were overcome by violent storms at sea. A water passage across the New World might shorten the trip to a year, and bring to the explorer who found the passage fame and, possibly, fortune.

Champlain, too, hoped that he would be the one to find this waterway, and that was why he had started up the Ottawa River.

A man called Nicolas de Vignau had travelled the area several years earlier, and had wintered with an Algonquin Indian tribe. He told Champlain that the river led to an ocean. Upon its shore, said Vignau, lay the remains of a shipwrecked English vessel. Champlain wondered if the ship could have belonged to Henry Hudson, an English explorer who drowned while exploring the bay which was to bear his name. Hudson, too, had been searching for the Northwest Passage.

Champlain asked the young man who so vividly described this shipwreck to accompany him on his journey.

Nicolas must have been a strange man. He agreed to go along

even though he knew that his story was not true. He had lived
with the Algonquins at Allumette Lake, not far from the twin falls,
but he had never travelled farther, and had certainly never seen a
shipwreck on the banks of an ocean. He must have known that his
lie would be discovered yet he agreed to show Champlain where
this mythical sea would be. By the time the little canoeing company
had reached the falls Nicolas must have been growing very uneasy.

Champlain admired the falls enough to note them in his diary,
but he did not give them a name. This was done by later explorers,
who also saw the falls' resemblance to graceful drapery, and who
gave them the name *Rideau,* which is the French word for curtain.
Today the Falls can be admired without paddling to the middle of
the river as a viewing platform has been built along their east bank.

If Nicolas was getting worried as Champlain ordered the canoeing party to resume its paddling, he was given some time to think of a way out of his plight since another set of falls, just a mile or so ahead, greatly slowed their progress.

These falls, lower and wider than the first ones, had been given the name *Asticou* (As-tee-cu), the Indian word for a pot of boiling water. The falls did look like a huge boiling kettle, for the wild water had worn the surrounding rocks into a basin, from which clouds of spray rose like steam. Champlain translated the Indian name into the French word, *Chaudière*, and they are still called the Chaudière Falls today.

When they reached the falls, the canoeists were obliged to *portage*, a term coming from a French word meaning "to carry." We have taken the word into English too, but use it only to mean carrying a canoe overland between two waterways, or past an area where the water is too rough for paddling.

Portaging was a regular part of water travel at that time. Every canoeist who passed the Chaudière Falls had to portage. The Algonquins, whose enemies the Iroquois often tried to ambush them here, used to portage on a roundabout route through the Gatineau Hills on the north side of the river. It was their way of giving the Iroquois the slip, a trick which was often successful. Today Gatineau Park footpaths follow some of the same Indian trails.

Eventually, Nicolas de Vignau's time ran out. The canoeing party arrived at Allumette Lake where Nicolas had spent a winter. Nicolas never explained his lie; he kept silent to the end. Perhaps he was hoping that the Indians would not reveal that he had never been farther inland. But they did tell Champlain. For some reason, they had never liked Nicolas and when they heard how he had misled Champlain they were angry enough to want to kill him. We know that Champlain did not allow this, even though he, too, must have been disappointed and angry with the young man. We don't know what really happened to Nicolas. Some historians think he simply disappeared into the forest.

We do know that Champlain did not continue his trip upriver. There probably seemed to be no point in continuing just then. As well, he had lost his astrolabe, an instrument he needed for navigation. It was found more than two hundred years later by a fourteen-year-old boy as he walked over a ploughed field.

You can see what an astrolabe is like if you visit the statue of Champlain at Nepean Point. He is holding one at arm's length above his head (which is the wrong way to hold it – the sculptor made a mistake). Of course, that astrolabe is just a copy. Champlain's own is in a museum belonging to the New York Historical Society.

The river on which Champlain was travelling has had many names besides the name he gave it and its present name. The Indians called it *Kitchissippi*. English explorers referred to it as the Grand River. Much later, the French named it *Outaouais*, after a fur-trading Indian tribe who often travelled by in their canoes. The English mispronounced this French word and eventually the river became known by its mispronounced name, Ottawa.

Many years passed before anyone stopped to make a home near the two waterfalls that Champlain had admired. Most new Canadian settlers preferred to start homes near communities that were already established. It was safer to settle in groups and it was good to have someone nearby who could lend a hand with the difficult problems faced by a newcomer trying to carve a home out of the wilderness.

So the banks near the Chaudière Falls remained unsettled while the Ottawa River flowed on, serving as a water highway for the explorers, Indians, and fur traders who wanted to travel farther inland.

Among these travellers were the famous voyageurs.

Voyageur is a French word meaning traveller. The voyageurs paddled the rivers carrying massive packs of beaver pelts in their great canoes, thirty feet long and made of birch and cedar. The pelts were sold in Montreal and Quebec, where buyers from overseas gladly paid high prices in order to take them back to Europe. There the pelts were made into the felt hats which every well-dressed man, woman and child in the Seventeenth Century wanted to wear.

Voyageurs were a hardy lot. Years of paddling for eighteen hours a day, of carrying their heavy packs of furs and their eight-man canoes over portages, of sleeping and eating outdoors without even a tent for shelter, turned them into tough and skilful woodsmen.

Today you can walk along some of the same portages that were tramped by the voyageurs. In Brébeuf Park, just past the Chaudière Falls, walking along the paved footpath, it is easy to imagine you are a voyageur, weary from travel, bent under your heavy pack of furs and the weight of your canoe on your shoulders, the rapids roaring in your ears as you stumble over roots and rocks.

For two hundred years the banks of the Chaudière remained silent and forested. They were waiting for a very special type of settler, a settler who wasn't afraid of being isolated from other people, one who could see that a location near two waterfalls, where three rivers meet, would mean certain success for those brave enough to cut the first log of a settlement.

At last, such a settler came.

Philemon Wright

Philemon Wright was an American who had been born too late. He had a pioneer's spirit – he longed to turn wilderness into thriving communities. But by the late 1700s, when Philemon was living with his family of seven children in Woburn, Massachusetts, most of what was then the United States was already well past the pioneering stage. If Philemon wanted to be a frontiersman he would have to travel far into the west.

But there was another solution. He had heard that, in Canada, land was available for anyone willing to start a home in an unsettled part of the country. So Philemon had made three scouting trips to the province of Quebec, where he searched carefully for the right location. On the third trip he found it: the land on the north side of the Chaudière Falls, in the township of Hull.

Now, as he sat before the fire in his comfortable Woburn home, he hardly noticed the chatter of the children as he thought back to that last trip. How he and his men had studied the land, climbing many, many pine trees to get a good view! They had examined the river to make sure it was navigable. They had checked the trees, looking for the healthy growth that would indicate good soil. They had considered the falls, which could be harnessed for power to drive mills.

Still Philemon wondered. Was it really worth taking his family from this cozy, modern home to live in the middle of the forest eighty miles from the nearest neighbour? Was he expecting too much? The children were certainly anxious to go. Even the last doubter had become enthusiastic after Philemon had explained that five other families from Woburn would go along. Not all their friends would be left behind.

To the children – Phil, Bearie, Chrissy, Abbie, Christie, Mary, and Ruggles – the trip to this new home sounded as if it would be a great adventure. They would leave near the end of winter. Philemon had explained that it would be easier to push heavily loaded sleighs over the snow, especially where there were no roads, than it would be to try to force wagons over muddy or overgrown trails during the warmer seasons. And, he had pointed out, once they had reached the frozen river, it would be just like a paved road. But, most important, they would arrive in time to use every hour of spring planting and building time. No precious sunshine and warm weather would be wasted in travel.

They left Woburn on the 2nd of February, 1800: five families, twenty-five hired men, fourteen horses, eight oxen, seven sleighs. They took several barrels of pork, axes, hoes, and all the other supplies they thought they would need.

The children had expected the trip to be fun, and at first it was. They liked tramping through the woods, leading the animals, occasionally riding on the sleighs, and camping out at night. The children would help tie up the horses and oxen, gather wood for the fire, and clear away the snow. After supper, they prepared food to eat on the trail the following day. They all slept beneath the open sky; the women and children in the covered sleighs, the men near the fire.

But soon they began to find this kind of travelling was less fun than it had been at first. It was very cold and, because there was no river to use on this first part of the way, they had to go overland, cutting through the bushes and trees to make way for the sleighs. The children couldn't ride often because the sleighs were loaded with supplies. Plodding through the deep snow was exhausting for small feet.

It took them eighteen days to reach Montreal where they had a chance to rest. Then it was on again, until they came to the Ottawa River. Even here the journey was not as easy as the children had expected. The snow lay deep and the men could move ahead only a few steps at a time, cutting through the thick white cover with their axes, searching for the ice to test its strength.

During their first day on the river, the little group met an Indian with his wife and child. The child was being pulled on a little bark sleigh. This Indian, when Philemon was finally able to make him understand where the pioneers were going, was so worried that Philemon would get lost that he left his family in order to accompany the group to the Chaudière Falls, sixty-five miles ahead. With his guidance, six days later, the weary travellers arrived at the Falls! It was the 7th of March.

Perhaps it was a disappointment to the children, after struggling so far through the winter's cold, to arrive at a place which, to them, must have looked much like all the other places they had passed through. Certainly it was a lonely welcome they received. Not a single friendly face to greet them; no warmly-lit home. Only the steaming falls, thundering over the rocks; only the spooky, dark forest, snapping with cold.

Perhaps that night, as they sat around the campfire, one of the children asked Philemon why he had chosen this place for his village.

And Philemon, gazing into the flames and puffing on his pipe, may have explained that it was not at all like the others they had passed through. Their new home was special in many ways. The falls could be used to power sawmills and grist mills. The river would be their road to market, down which they would float their products. Philemon dreamed of sending huge loads of lumber down the river to the markets in Montreal. Lumber, he suspected, might become the settlement's best "cash crop," that is, the crop which would earn the most money.

So the children may have gone to bed that night with their enthusiasm renewed. Certainly they would need all they could muster to help them in the hard months ahead.

The settlers wasted no time in starting to clear the land, as we know from Philemon's accounts. He wrote that they cut the first tree immediately upon arrival, with the help of everyone who could use an axe. Land clearing continued through March, April, and May. Crops were planted as soon as space was cleared.

All but the very youngest children worked alongside the adults. In those days children of twelve years of age or so were considered capable of doing almost as much work as could a grownup. Even the very small ones would have had light tasks, such as weeding or gathering sticks.

Land clearing and planting were the most urgent tasks that first year. There was no time to build more than simple log cabins. But each year after that buildings were added, and soon the new settlement looked like a well-established village. By the time the children were grown there were streets, a hotel, a ferry, and all the conveniences found in most towns in those days.

When Philemon first bought the land it was called the Township of Hull, but as the settlement grew, the village began to be called Wrightstown, Wrightsville, or some other variation with "Wright" in it and the falls were called Columbia Falls. Today we use the earlier names: Hull and Chaudière Falls.

Philemon's dream of sending lumber down the Ottawa River to Montreal and Quebec eventually came true. At first nobody believed he would be able to force loads of lumber over the many falls and rapids along the way but Philemon was not a man to give up easily. He and his sons built special chutes, much like playground slides, over or beside the difficult places along the river. Then they fastened their loads of lumber to large rafts. The rafts would slide down the chutes, by-passing the rapids.

At first it took several months for Philemon's lumber to reach Montreal, but, after much practice, he and his sons learned to get the rafts to market in less than a month.

Philemon's lumbering success became very important to the area. For many years it remained the chief industry along the Ottawa. Today not so much lumbering is done, but you can still see masses of logs corralled in the river above the Chaudière Falls, waiting to be turned into wood products in the one mill still remaining.

Although Philemon's community grew every year, not many settlers considered crossing the river to start another on the opposite side. So, while the north bank buzzed with activity, the south side, where Ottawa is today, remained almost as quiet as it had been in Champlain's time.

Then a stranger came, and changed all that forever.

Colonel By and the Rideau Canal

The stranger was Colonel John By, an engineer sent from England on a special assignment.

In 1776, fifty years before Colonel By set foot in Wrightstown, the English colonies just south of Canada had won a war against England and had become an independent nation, the United States of America.

In the years during and after this war, which was called the American Revolution, there was considerable ill-feeling between Canadian colonists and Americans. Most Canadians felt that the Americans should not have turned against Britain, their mother-land, and most Americans looked upon Canadians as cowards, almost traitors, for refusing to join their revolution. Besides, the many American colonists who had not wanted to join the revolution had moved to Canada, and this added to the new nation's resentment of its northern neighbour.

Feelings were so strong that England feared the United States might begin another war to force the Canadians to join them by taking over their lands. In such a war, one of the first American moves might be to blockade the St. Lawrence River. This would cut off the supply route for one of the most important English forts in Canada, Fort Henry at Kingston.

For years the provincial governments in Upper and Lower Canada discussed the need to strengthen their defence of the St. Lawrence and Kingston, but there was little money available to build forts and ships so nothing was done. In 1812, as had been expected for so long, England and the United States went to war again. The war ended in 1815, without the dreaded blockade of the St. Lawrence. For some unknown reason, the American plans to do so were never carried out. England realized, however, that she might not be so lucky next time and decided to solve the St. Lawrence problem at her own expense.

This is where Colonel By came in. He was to supervise the building of a canal from Ottawa to Kingston which would connect the Ottawa River and Lake Ontario. The canal would be approximately one hundred and twenty–five miles long. You can see from the map that this would provide another supply route for the Kingston fort.

Colonel By arrived in Wrightstown on September 21st, 1826. The town by then had a hotel, an armoury, three churches, and a school or two. Philemon Wright, who was nearly seventy years old, lived in a large stone house near the Chaudière Falls. He and Colonel By became friends at once.

By had a huge task ahead of him, and he set to work immediately. Except for a few settlers who owned land there, the southern bank of the Ottawa River was almost a wilderness. The Colonel examined the area carefully before choosing a site for the entrance to the canal. Along with his superior officer, the Earl of Dalhousie, he decided upon a small cove east of the large bluff about a mile below the Chaudière Falls.

Colonel By then had to prepare for the many workers who would have to be hired. He divided two pieces of land, both near the bank of the river, into lots. One group of lots was on the high bluff, and this he named Upper Town. The other group, lying east of the bluff, he named Lower Town. Both sets of lots were to be rented to the workers for their houses.

The Colonel then needed a survey of the land between Ottawa and Kingston, in order to plan a canal route which would be as simple as possible to construct. This task he gave to John MacTaggart, one of his engineers. MacTaggart later wrote a book, *Three Years in Canada*, in which he described the difficulties of the assignment.

The surveying party set out in October, crawling on their hands and knees much of the time, through mucky swamp water. The wilderness was so densely overgrown with trees and vines that climbing a tree was no help in determining the lay of the land. In the end they had to postpone their trip until winter, when at least they could walk upright on the frozen, snow-covered muck. Even then, when the surveying recommenced in December, the woods were so dark and thick that the men could not see more than five feet ahead. MacTaggart wrote that, to keep from losing each other, they would send one man ahead for about half a mile. He would then wait for the rest, while blowing a horn. The others would catch up by moving towards the sound.

At night they would cook chunks of pork over a campfire while passing round a single mug of tea. Then, huddled together for warmth, feet nearest the fire, they would sleep. If one wanted to turn over he would call out, "Spoon!", and they would all turn over together. When they awoke, they often found their hair frozen to the ground!

You can get an idea of how slow this surveying process was when you consider that the group spent their Christmas Day at Hog's Back Falls, having left the bank of the Ottawa on December 20th. Today a bicyclist, leaving from the same area, can reach Hog's Back in forty minutes.

Even so, by the following year the Colonel was ready to start construction of the canal. Since the local population was small to begin with, and since very few of the workers who lived nearby were trained for canal building, Colonel By had to send for workers from Europe. Among those who came to work were two companies of the Royal Sappers and Miners, British regiments, made up of eighty soldiers per company. They had to live in canvas tents until their barracks were erected on the bluff, soon to be known as Barracks Hill. Many of these men stayed on to farm the hundred acres of land which Colonel By arranged for each of them to be given when the canal was complete and they were discharged from the army.

With so many canal workers to accommodate, Upper and Lower Town were soon filled with houses – one hundred and fifty were built within the first two years. And just as Philemon's little community had come to be known as Wrightstown, the new community on the opposite side of the river became known as Bytown.

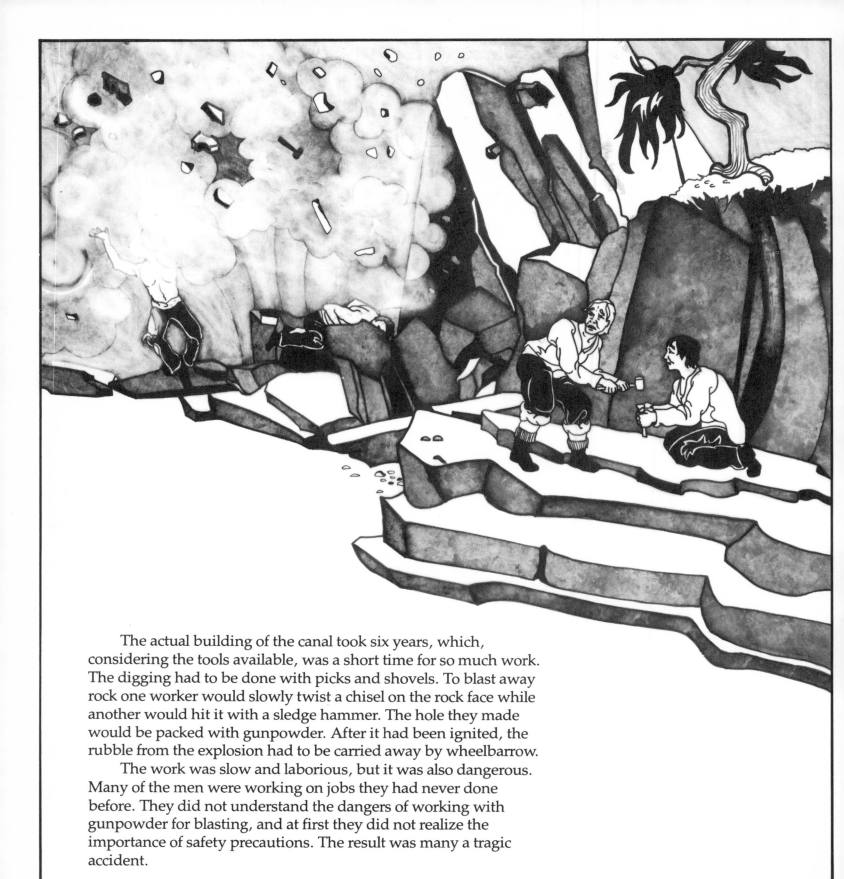

The actual building of the canal took six years, which, considering the tools available, was a short time for so much work. The digging had to be done with picks and shovels. To blast away rock one worker would slowly twist a chisel on the rock face while another would hit it with a sledge hammer. The hole they made would be packed with gunpowder. After it had been ignited, the rubble from the explosion had to be carried away by wheelbarrow.

The work was slow and laborious, but it was also dangerous. Many of the men were working on jobs they had never done before. They did not understand the dangers of working with gunpowder for blasting, and at first they did not realize the importance of safety precautions. The result was many a tragic accident.

There was another danger to which everyone succumbed at one time or another: swamp fever. Building the canal meant digging through large areas of swamp. Something about these swamps was very unhealthy, for when the workers were toiling in the swamp mud they often became deathly ill.

One of the worst places for swamp fever was Cranberry Lake, near Kingston. It was really a bog, but was called a lake after dams had been built across it to retain the water. In summer, a blue mist hung over it. It was beautiful but unhealthy, the area reeking, writes MacTaggart, like the carcass of a dead animal.

Once, during an inspection tour, Colonel By's canoe became grounded in this smelly place. When his men jumped overboard to free it, they sank to their waists in the stinking mud. Soon after all but two of the men died of the fever and Colonel By became so ill it was feared he would die as well. But he was a tough man and he recovered, although it is thought that his death several years later was partly a result of his being weakened by this attack. Today we think the fever was a form of malaria. Only the Indians were immune to it.

At last, in 1832, the canal was completed. Colonel By must surely have been looking forward to some reward for his great achievement. Some people think he was hoping to be knighted. Instead, he was asked to appear before a court of enquiry in England. The English officials were disturbed because the canal had cost more than they had first thought it would. They suspected that the Colonel had cheated them, keeping some of the extra money for himself.

The enquiry found the Colonel innocent. Still, he was given no reward for his great work. In fact people avoided him. It happens that way sometimes – even if someone is proven innocent of a crime, people wonder if he was *really* guilty. So no one spoke on the Colonel's behalf. Perhaps because so few people in England saw the canal, or the Canadian wilderness, they did not understand what a great service Colonel By had performed.

Disappointed and hurt, Colonel By retired to a farm in the English countryside. His health was weakened by the hardships of his years in Canada. Four lonely, bitter years later, he died.

Today there are many fond reminders of the Colonel in Ottawa. A parkway which follows one side of the canal is named Colonel By Drive. There is a monument erected in his memory in Major's Hill Park, near the spot where he had built his own house. Byward Market, where farmers sell their fruits and vegetables on the street, is named after him. You can visit a building filled with Colonel By's belongings. It is at the foot of the canal, beside the first locks. The Colonel's men built it to store their food and tools. We call it the Bytown Museum.

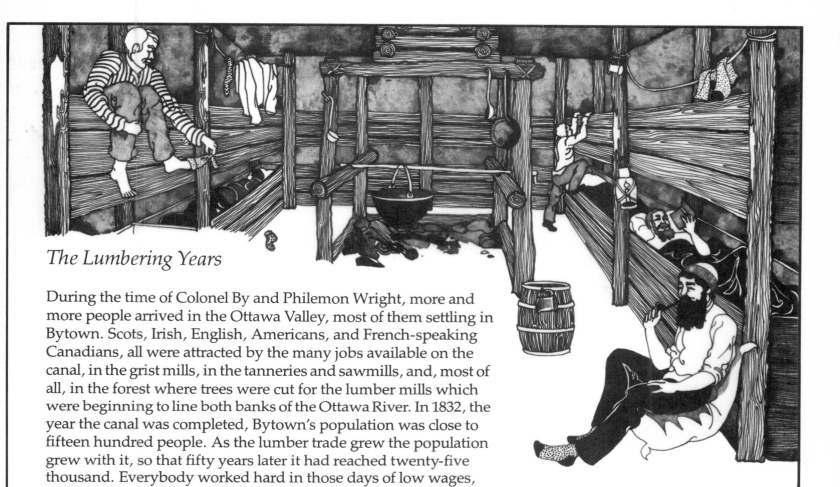

The Lumbering Years

During the time of Colonel By and Philemon Wright, more and more people arrived in the Ottawa Valley, most of them settling in Bytown. Scots, Irish, English, Americans, and French-speaking Canadians, all were attracted by the many jobs available on the canal, in the grist mills, in the tanneries and sawmills, and, most of all, in the forest where trees were cut for the lumber mills which were beginning to line both banks of the Ottawa River. In 1832, the year the canal was completed, Bytown's population was close to fifteen hundred people. As the lumber trade grew the population grew with it, so that fifty years later it had reached twenty-five thousand. Everybody worked hard in those days of low wages, long hours, and poor working conditions, but the men who made their living by logging surely chose the most difficult job of all!

Philemon Wright and his sons, the first men to cut Gatineau logs for an income, did not have to go far from home for their lumber. But the men who were hired by the lumber companies in later years had to move into the forest so far from their homes that it was more sensible to live there for the logging season.

The men lived in shanties built of logs, dovetailed at the corners. Cracks between them were filled with mud outside and moss inside. The water-tight roofs were hollowed-out *scoops,* made from half-trunks, and laid so that the curved top of one scoop lay inside the hollowed-out portion of the next one. There was one door but usually no windows. Light and air came from an opening in the centre of the roof, directly above the large cooking fire. This fire, called *camboose,* from a Dutch word meaning a place where food is prepared, burned constantly in a fireplace made from rocks and fine sand. Its square, wooden chimney went straight up through the hole in the roof. Double-decker bunks, with spruce boughs for mattresses, lined the walls, allowing the men to sleep with their feet towards the fire.

The loggers arrived at the camp in late autumn. They had a long, hard season ahead of them. To begin work at six A.M. the men had to be up by five. Time and the cold weather discouraged them from washing much; showers, tubs and hot water were unheard of in the camp. Beans, home-made bread (both baked in the hot sand of the camboose), and strong tea made up the first meal of the day. Then it was off to the logging site, to chop, saw, and haul logs until sundown. In the Gatineau forest the winter sun could set as early as mid-afternoon so they had to work fast. Back at the shanty again supper would usually consist of more beans, bread, and tea. When a supply wagon could get in, pork, beef, butter, dried apples, sugar, and even fish, were available to break the monotony.

The shantymen worked six days a week. Saturday night was reserved for entertainment–the men knew they could sleep late the following day. Checkers and cards, singing and dancing, all accompanied by the fiddle or a mouth organ, created a feeling of fellowship. Sundays were days of rest. Sometimes a visiting minister or, more often, a priest, would hold a church service. It must have been a lonely life, spending day after day for months with the same men, always knowing that the next day would be as full of the same monotonous work as the last. Lying on his bunk, watching the wet socks and shirts drying by the fire, listening to the snores of his comrades, the logger must have longed for his wife and family, whom he would not see again until summer.

As spring approached the men began to grow restless. With the arrival of the melting ice and snows would come the most dangerous, the most back-breaking, and the most thrilling time of all: the time when the logs must be guided down the rivers to the sawmills, the time they called "the drive."

All winter the loggers had felled trees and, using horses and oxen, hauled them to the nearest river or stream that flowed into the mighty Ottawa. There the logs were piled right on the ice, and there the logs had remained until the ice began to thaw. The loggers grew anxious as the ice began to crack. They were waiting for the priests and ministers who would bless them and pray for them before they began their dangerous work.

At last it was time for the drive! Imagine the river, so filled with logs the water was barely visible. Imagine the logs, spinning, rolling, tossing and tumbling in the fast-moving waters of a wild river in spring flood!

The loggers, brandishing pike poles, had to run along the banks, making sure the logs flowed freely. Then from somewhere along the bank would come the dreaded shout, "Jam!" Jam! the word that would send a shiver of fear into a logger's heart, a word which meant that, somehow, among the fast-flowing logs in the river, one log had become caught, wedged, perhaps, against a rock. Behind it, the others would begin a relentless pile-up, like a giant beaver dam taking shape in the river.

It was the loggers' nightmare. They knew that one of them must free the jam, and one day it could cost him his life. So dangerous was this part of the logger's job that, in later years, dynamite was sometimes used to break the jam. But the men thought using dynamite was a cowardly way out, and, in those days especially, being a coward was a worse fate, for most men, than death itself.

And so one or two of the loggers would have to walk out onto
the jam where they had to poke, push, and pull at the bewildering
jumble of logs until they had found the key log–the one causing the
jam. Then it was "all hands and the cook," heaving and pulling to
free the jammed log. And when the jam loosened, the men had to
be quick to spring out of the way of the leaping logs, hurtled up in all
directions by the suddenly released pressure. Many a sad lumbering song tells of the unlucky loggers who had not paid attention to
the warning groans and creaks of a jam about to break loose.

Once the logs had reached the Ottawa River they had to be sent
to Montreal and Quebec. But they couldn't simply float down as
loose sticks. They had to be sorted and bound together before they
could be sold for shipbuilding, houses, paper and many other uses.

Sorting was done by examining the timber mark on each log.
This mark was a brand and each brand belonged to one company.
The logging companies corralled their logs into booms, floating
fences in the river, made from a chain of logs, then sorted them into
piles of equal sizes in order to prepare them for "rafting."

Rafting meant sending huge rafts made up of cribs down the river. Cribs were small platforms, about fifty feet long and twenty-five feet wide, made from logs. They were bound together into one gigantic raft which could contain as many as two hundred cribs. Because crews were going to live on them the rafts contained a cookery crib outfitted with a sand oven over which hung the cook pots. There were bunk houses for the fifty-man crew and over them flew the company pennant.

These clumsy rafts, like wooden blankets, were powered by oars or "sweeps," and on windy days in broad stretches of water by sails. Sometimes, in slow water, they had to be "kedged." This meant that the anchor was thrown far ahead, and then, by a pulley

attached to the anchor's rope, the raft was hauled up to the anchor, after which the whole process was repeated. By the 1840s tug boats were in use and kedging was no longer necessary.

Whenever the water was too wild to travel on, the rafts had to be taken apart and carried overland, or else sent, crib by crib, down a chute similar to the one built by the Wrights. Of course, the whole raft had to be reassembled as soon as smooth water was reached.

When the logs had been delivered to the market in Quebec, where the timber was sold to merchants from Europe, the drivers were free to return to their families and spend the summer months farming their small properties.

But soon they would be back at the shanties again.

Bytown Changes Its Name

Bytown continued to grow because of the lumber mills and factories which provided work there. By 1855, when the population had passed eight thousand, it was large enough to become a city.

The inhabitants felt that their city should no longer have a name with the word "town" at the end of it. Many names were suggested: Sydenham, after the governor; Aberdeen, in honour of the Count of that name; Queensburg, to please Queen Victoria.

Unable to choose among so many, the people finally turned to an historical source. The *Outaouais* Indians still passed by on the river, carrying their cargoes of furs. So Bytown became Ottawa, the English version of *Outaouais*. The French spelling is used today as the name of a large district on the Quebec side of the Ottawa River.

Life in Early Ottawa

You had to be both brave and strong to live in Ottawa during the first few years after it changed its name. It was a rough, tough town.

To understand why there was so much violence, it is necessary to know a little about the kind of people who worked in Bytown, and what their living conditions were like.

The many different nationalities that made up the population were often intolerant of one another. Scotsmen were not particularly fond of Irishmen or French-speaking Canadians, nor were the Irish and French very friendly with the Scots or with each other. Partly this was because of national pride, partly because of religious prejudice, and partly it was because of fear: each group thought that another group might take over its jobs.

In addition to these problems, all of the workers shared living conditions which were bound to make for short tempers. Most of them had to live in the poor, shabby, crowded little shanties which had sprung up in Lower Town and near the mills. Working hours were long in those days, often from sun-up to sundown, in noisy, crowded mills which had none of the comforts of today's sleek factories. Wages were very low, so that a hard day's work still gave people no hope of buying the things which could have made life more pleasant.

Fights started easily, often at the slightest excuse and, whenever the men who had spent long months in the lumber camps came to town, there was added trouble. Having just been paid, and finally having a place to spend the money, these loggers often went wild. The first stop would be the local bar, followed by every other bar they could reach before their money ran out. By that time they were drunk and happy to use any excuse for some excitement. This often came in the form of a brawl.

The Saturday fights, held then because the workers had the afternoon off, took place in a special fighting ring near Mosgrove Street (Freiman Street today). This ring had for years been the recognised place for settling disputes. In Bytown's early days, it had been almost the only place to fight. Fights at work or on the streets were not common then. Ring fights were conducted according to rules, and were often the main source of entertainment, although occasionally the audience became over-enthusiastic and began fighting too.

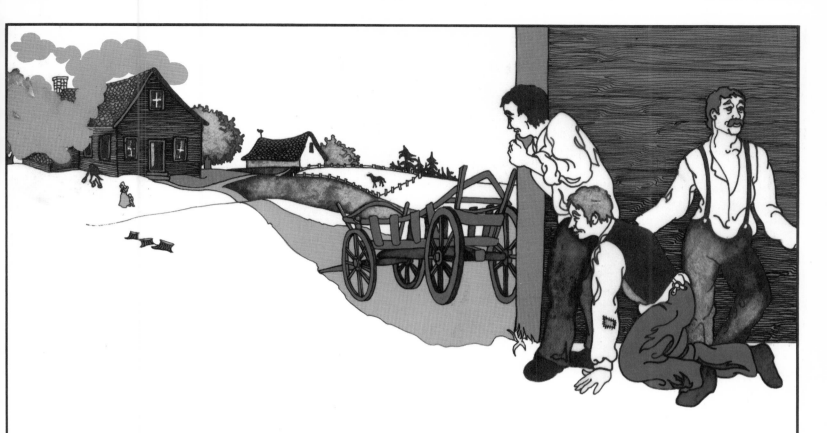

There are those who blame the Shiners for being the main cause of violence in those early years. They were Irishmen who had been brought to this country to work in the mills. Some people say the name was supposed to indicate that they shone above everybody else. Others say it came from the French word *cheneurs*, because *chêne* means oak, and these men used oak for building bridges. The word soon became mispronounced as "shiners." There are also those who suggest they got the name because they gave so many black eyes.

Their chief enemies were the French-speaking Canadians who worked in the mills. Their experience in this type of work meant that they were often hired instead of the Shiners. The Irishmen would play all kinds of tricks on the French. They would steal their furniture and leave it in the snow. They would set fire to their houses. Spoiling wells, interfering with funerals, nothing was too sacred for the Shiners.

At first the French put up with a good deal of this treatment, but eventually they began to fight back and often local troops had to be summoned.

Because of all the brawling, Ottawa was considered a city to avoid by people who lived elsewhere. However, in 1858 Ottawa received an honour which eventually helped change both other people's attitudes, and the character of the city itself.

A Capital City

While Ottawa and Wrightstown were growing into cities, the provinces of Lower Canada, now called Quebec, and Upper Canada, now called Ontario, were growing too.

Eventually they decided to join together, forming the United Province of Canada. Each had had its own capital city, but now a new capital would be needed.

Several cities in both provinces were anxious for the honour. Kingston, Montreal, Quebec City, Toronto and Ottawa were all in the running. Of them all it was thought that brawling Ottawa had the least chance of success.

Kingston was the first city to bear the title. It was an English-speaking city, however, which made life very difficult for those legislators who spoke only French.

For this reason, the capital was changed to Montreal, an ideal choice, since both languages were common there. But Montreal had a riot during which the Parliament buildings were burned, and the government, afraid that it might happen again, did not like to risk losing a second group of buildings. So the capital was changed again.

This time the choice was Toronto. But once again there was
the problem of an English-speaking city. The only fair solution
seemed to be to let a French-speaking city, Quebec, take turns with
Toronto every four years. The solution was not satisfactory. Moving
documents and government employees every four years turned
out to be too much of a nuisance.

Finally the government turned to Queen Victoria for help. She was asked to choose the capital city for the new Province. Naturally, all the contenders sent her information showing why, clearly, their city was the only choice.

The Queen did not make a hasty decision. She carefully considered the alternatives. One letter she examined was written by Sir Edmund Head, the Governor General. He felt Ottawa should be chosen for several reasons:

Firstly, the city was situated at the border of the united provinces, with a bridge joining them.

Secondly, several languages were common in the city: no one
could complain that the city was exclusively French – or English –
speaking.

Thirdly, Ottawa was not likely to be attacked. Montreal or
Kingston would have to be captured first, because it was between
those two well-protected cities.

Some people say that it was this letter which influenced the
Queen. Others say she was influenced by some watercolour
sketches of the cliffs above the Ottawa River. We can't be sure what
made her decide, but on January 1, 1858, the Queen's choice was
announced.

Ottawa was to be the capital!

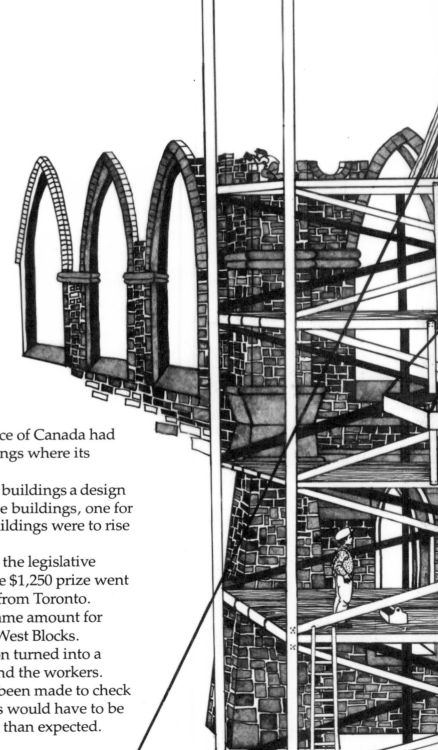

The Parliament Buildings

Now that the government of the United Province of Canada had a capital city in which to meet, it needed buildings where its Parliament could convene.

To find the most attractive style for the new buildings a design contest was held. Contestants were to plan three buildings, one for legislative meetings and two for offices. The buildings were to rise on Barracks Hill, overlooking the Ottawa River.

By August, winners had been chosen. For the legislative building, soon to be called the Centre Block, the $1,250 prize went to Thomas Fuller and Chilion Jones, architects from Toronto. Frederick Stent and Augustus Laver won the same amount for their office buildings, now called the East and West Blocks.

Construction began in December, and soon turned into a nightmare for the government, the planners, and the workers. Because of poor planning, no test borings had been made to check the depth of the rock upon which the buildings would have to be constructed, and the men had to dig far deeper than expected.

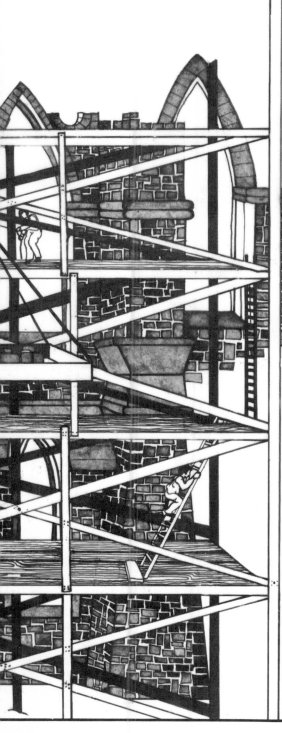

Obtaining the stone from which the buildings were to be built was expensive and difficult, and no heating system had been planned. Finally, all these delays, which added to the costs of construction, resulted in the government's running out of money to pay the workers and contractors, and, two years after it had begun, all construction was stopped.

The work stoppage caused a great deal of hardship for the workers, especially those who had come from Europe just to work on the Parliament Buildings. They suddenly had to find other work in a strange country. To do so, most of them had to move to other parts of Canada or to the United States. In the end, the government came up with a plan to finish as much of the work as was absolutely necessary, so as many workers as could be located were rehired.

By 1865, most of the construction was completed except for the library. The tower was to be finished later. The meeting rooms and offices were ready and by October of 1865 the first government employees began to arrive.

In 1866 the first Parliamentary session was held in the legislative chamber. Already nearly three hundred civil servants were living in Ottawa. In 1867 the chamber had to be enlarged because two more provinces, Nova Scotia and New Brunswick, had decided to join the national family at the time of Confederation.

In 1916, a fire demolished the Centre Block. Only the library was saved, thanks to a quick-thinking person who closed the big iron doors. The government moved to the Victoria Museum (now the Museum of Man) for a four-year stay while its old home was being rebuilt.

A new Centre Block was designed by John Pearson and was ready by 1920 for the return of Parliament, although some work still had to be done. In 1927, the Peace Tower was completed. Decorative stone carving is still being worked on today in some parts of the building.

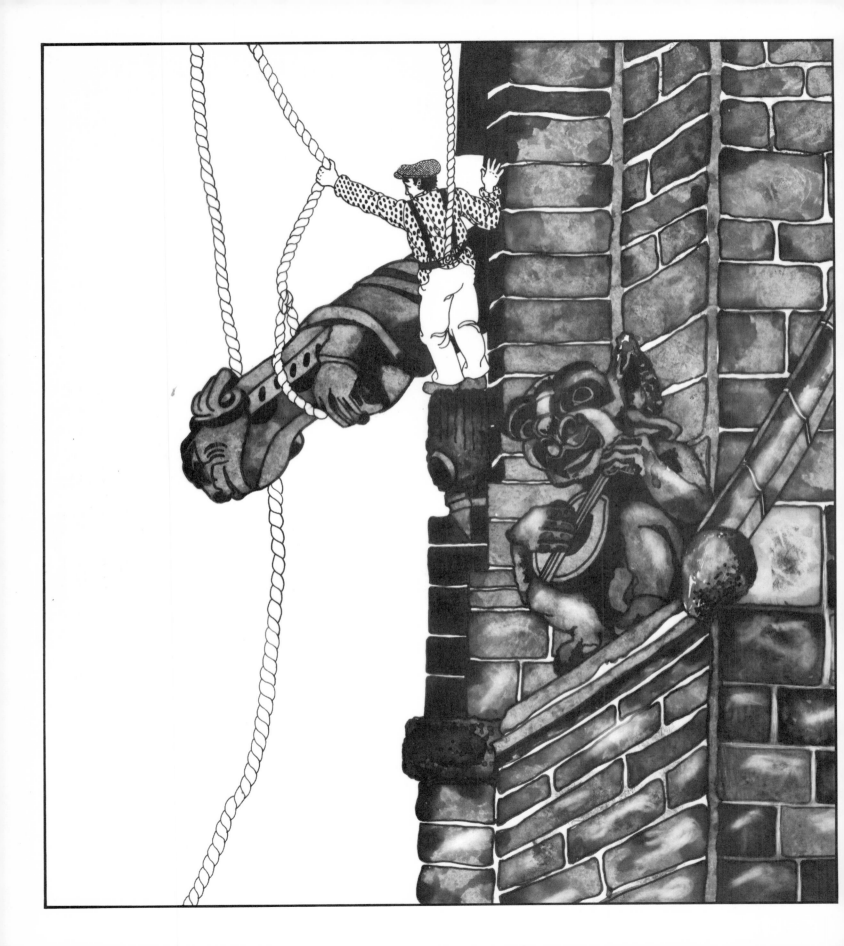

The Parliament Buildings are delightful to visit. On a guided tour you will be shown fossils in the limestone used for the inside walls. You will see the grey, black and green marble floors, and wood trim of white oak and pine, which is particularly beautiful in the library.

If you climb the Peace Tower you will have north, south, east, and west views of the Capital and the Gatineau Hills, and a chance to examine the old-fashioned workings of the Peace Tower clock. Today a modern motor turns the hands and the old one is just for show.

You will also see where Parliament does its work, in the House of Commons and Senate chambers. One is a luxurious red, the other a cool, elegant green. The stained glass windows in the House of Commons chamber are breathtaking. And if you come when Parliament is in session, you may watch the Members of Parliament, our lawmakers, at work.

The Federal Capital

At the time that Queen Victoria chose Ottawa to be the capital of the United Province of Canada she had many subjects living in other parts of this country. By 1867 the people of Nova Scotia and New Brunswick had decided to join the United Province to form the Dominion of Canada. The new Dominion needed a capital and since the fine new Parliament Buildings were in Ottawa already, the town that Colonel By had built remained a capital city.

In 1867 Ottawa was still a small city. It had a few stone buildings as well as the Parliament Buildings. Its main industry was still lumbering. Sawmills and papermills cluttered the riverbanks. Along the Rideau Canal were warehouses and construction sites. The first railways were being built and many miles of track quickly spread through the city.

By the end of the century the first plans were being made to turn Ottawa into a fine city of parks and beautiful buildings, a worthy capital for our growing nation.

Six more provinces were to join the Dominion: Manitoba in 1870; British Columbia in 1871; Prince Edward Island in 1873 and Saskatchewan and Alberta in 1905. It was not until 1949, eighty-two years after Confederation, that Newfoundland became a part of Canada. With each enlargement of the Dominion, Ottawa remained the capital, but the greatest day in Ottawa's story must surely have been the first Dominion Day!

The First Dominion Day

Canada became a nation on July 1st, 1867. Our first Prime Minister was Sir John A. Macdonald.

The great day was a Monday. At dawn one hundred and one guns fired their salute to tell Canadians that history was being made. At the sound of the guns a huge bonfire was lit on Nepean Point and bells rang all over the city to spread the news. Everyone in Ottawa seemed to be having a party that day. Imagine the ladies in their crinolines and ribbons, the gentlemen in fine linen and handsome uniforms, as they went to tea-parties, dinner-parties, garden-parties and dances, all through the hot summer day. Ottawa knew it had become part of the international community when the first ever trans-Atlantic cable arrived in the city with a message from Queen Victoria.

In the evening, everyone gathered in front of the Parliament Buildings for the grand display of fireworks that ended the day.

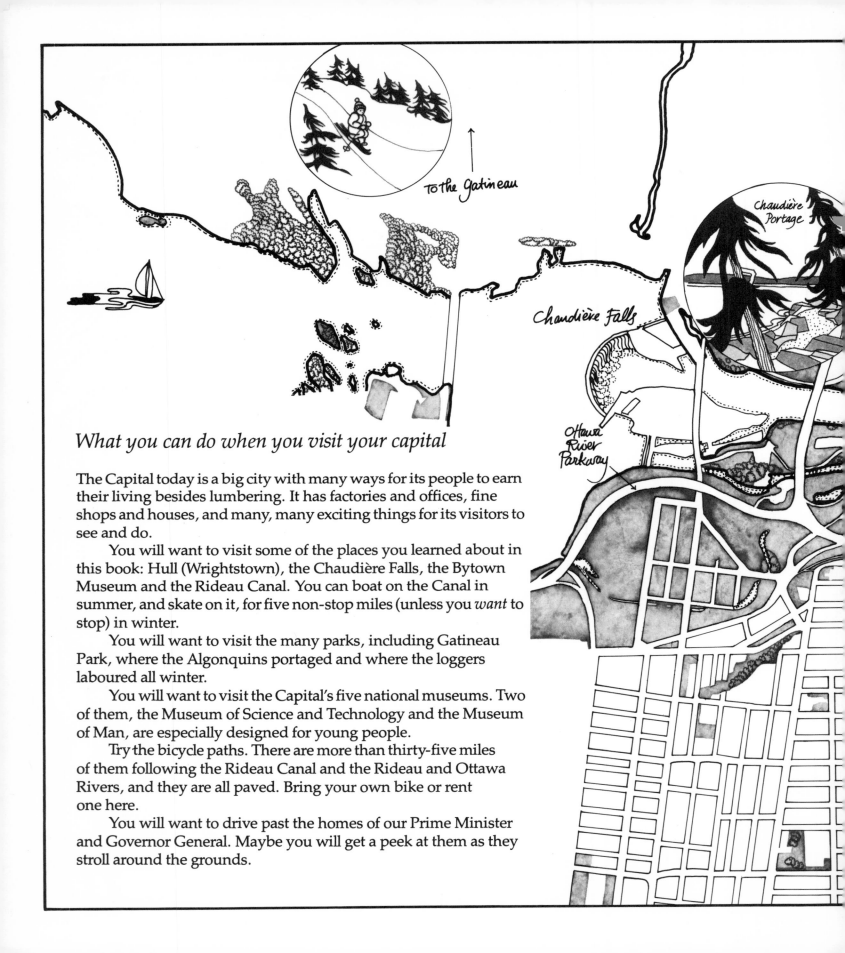

What you can do when you visit your capital

The Capital today is a big city with many ways for its people to earn their living besides lumbering. It has factories and offices, fine shops and houses, and many, many exciting things for its visitors to see and do.

You will want to visit some of the places you learned about in this book: Hull (Wrightstown), the Chaudière Falls, the Bytown Museum and the Rideau Canal. You can boat on the Canal in summer, and skate on it, for five non-stop miles (unless you *want* to stop) in winter.

You will want to visit the many parks, including Gatineau Park, where the Algonquins portaged and where the loggers laboured all winter.

You will want to visit the Capital's five national museums. Two of them, the Museum of Science and Technology and the Museum of Man, are especially designed for young people.

Try the bicycle paths. There are more than thirty-five miles of them following the Rideau Canal and the Rideau and Ottawa Rivers, and they are all paved. Bring your own bike or rent one here.

You will want to drive past the homes of our Prime Minister and Governor General. Maybe you will get a peek at them as they stroll around the grounds.

Rideau Falls

24 Sussex Drive

City Hall

Rideau Hall

Ottawa River

Rideau River

Sussex Drive

Mint

Nepean Point

War Museum

Rideau Canal

Byward Market

Sparks Street Mall

Parliament Hill

National Arts Centre

University of Ottawa

If you come when Parliament is in session (during the fall, winter, and spring months, except for Christmas and Easter recesses), go to the Green Chamber to watch the men and women who make our nation's laws discuss and plan what is best for our country. Don't be shy – they would *like* to have you visit!

There are many things for you to do so try to stay several days to be sure you don't miss anything.

And remember, it is *your* Capital – come and see it soon!

The Author

Nadja Corkum is a freelance writer, sometime newspaper correspondent, and a magazine editor. She spent six years teaching in private and public schools. Born in Nova Scotia, she now resides in Ottawa.

The Illustrator

Emma Hesse is a freelance book designer and illustrator. A graduate of Toronto's Ontario College of Art, she was born in Niagara Falls and presently works and lives in Toronto.